Mercury in Scorpio

Sara Filipiak

BookLeaf
Publishing

India | USA | UK

Presentation by *BookLeaf Publishing*

Web: www.bookleafpub.com

E-mail: info@bookleafpub.com

ISBN: 9789358734775

First edition 2023

DEDICATION

This book of poems I dedicate to the ones we lost too soon. Your absence is felt everyday.

P.S…

I'll always use my words as a balm to soothe my broken heart from the pain of loss.

PREFACE

"Throw roses into the abyss and say: 'here is my thanks to the monster who didn't succeed in swallowing me alive."

Friedrich Nietzsche

Past

I won't mourn
for you.
I won't reach
for you.
You were never a
sure thing. I
haven't
lost anything.

"You're either running free or running scared."

Your books are
your chasers. Your drinks
are your drugs. You're a
lonely nightmare running
away from love.

Bro

He's lost from
me
like fog in the
dead of night
City
streets.

Pops

In the morning, it wakes me
up like I died in a
nightmare. I
instantly rise dripping
with sweat. I feel lost enough
as it is. I can't
let it win. He wouldn't
want me to give
in. If he
was here all
this grief would
disappear. And I
would feel whole
again.

Fire & Ice Roses

5

Here now in
this time. I keep roses
even when they die. It reminds me
that I'm still alive even when
I feel dead inside.

Like a flower pressed
in the book of
time, the memories reside,
frozen in my mind.

Eternal Dagger

At any given moment, I can
be brought to
my knees, dagger through
the side, shadows
suffocating the mind. You
never see it
coming like vulgar
insulating words rolling
off the tongue, it
takes jabs
trying to overpower you. Memories
are sweet like
violets and sometimes
razor
sharp like thorns.

"Every day is exactly the same." (NIN song)

Numbness that's stone
cold like a marble
statue. Nothing can exist
there. Absence makes the
heartbeat bitter, and the only
way out is through. I have
nothing else to
write. Misery is making
me miserable tonight.

Father's Day

I stopped scrolling on IG today
is that day when all the daddy
posts are posted. No post
from me. It's easier to
ignore because the
burning anger fills
in the space of his memory.

Present

Your absence has
made me grey like a
rainstorm that never
ends. When it stops, it
starts again. I'm lost
without you.

Devotion/Future Lover

Drowning in love feels
like a gentle but firm
grip around your throat.
You're smiling, enjoying
every minute of it, letting go
of control. Deep within, you
know he would die for
you. And that
this moment
was worth waiting for.

Past Lives

I was already etching
your name into
my wrist. I
don't know
you yet but
I will. When I see
you, I'll know. Like
trains, the universe is
bringing you home. Then you'll
see me too.

Star Crossed

Tiny fragments of
my soul is missing. If I could
find you, I would find
myself.

I
spot
you. I can see my
soul too! Together they
sparkle like a
Quartz necklace
dangling in the
night sky forever.

Ouroboros

Look at those
clouds; they
could remind me of pink
snake scales. The sky is shedding, as am I. A full
circle moment
sign. Translated
in the sky, for my heart/mind.

Angel Kisses

I broke another mirror again,
shiny truth serum. I don't
want my eyes
wide open to see
it. I catch myself
staring, and I notice my
dimples. I smile back,
your face arrives. It's
like I never said
goodbye.

Little Things

I can count on both hands things I'm grateful
for…

One, all the pets are asleep and cozy in their
beds.
Two, the beautiful ombré orange sherbet sunrise
I witnessed from my kitchen window.
Three, doing my breath work and affirmations.
Four, "Enjoy the Silence" played , as I was
walking into my favorite coffee shop.
Five, being healthy and able to be on the wild
ride called life, even when it sucks.

Now,
slowly my eyes become
weights. Sinking into
my marshmallow bed, I drift
off. In the morning,
my heart is always filled
with gratefulness.

Goodbye M.B

At any moment we
could
fall apart. I'm not the
one that's going
to hold
you when the waves of
grief crash through
you. You'll
be in good hands. And
i'll wish on
every star
for your happiness to burn
forever true. I would
die
for you,
so that you may
fall in
the loving arms
of another.

Today

Today is
full of goodbyes. The
first goodbye was like
a sigh. And my wave
showed reverence. The
second goodbye surprised me like
I was a deer in the
headlights. I didn't
wave. I just said aloud
"Goodbye."p

Wake Up

It strikes me, to the core, to hear about loss. My insides shake all around like a magic 8-ball. Pain rushes to my face like a slap across the cheek. I think of all the times when my mind was in a black hole and not wanting to feel a damn thing. I'll push back the darkness like a warrior. I understand the reason for my existence, to be a light for the world. Hearing about loss, it whispers to me, " Wake up! You're alive! So live!"